One-Dimensional Woman

Nina Power

BOOKS

Winchester, UK
Washington, USA

One-Dimensional
Woman

First published by O Books, 2009
O Books is an imprint of John Hunt Publishing Ltd., The Bothy, Deershot Lodge, Park Lane, Ropley,
Hants, SO24 0BE, UK
office1@o-books.net
www.o-books.net

Distribution in:

UK and Europe
Orca Book Services
orders@orcabookservices.co.uk
Tel: 01202 665432 Fax: 01202 666219
Int. code (44)

USA and Canada
NBN
custserv@nbnbooks.com
Tel: 1 800 462 6420 Fax: 1 800 338 4550

Australia and New Zealand
Brumby Books
sales@brumbybooks.com.au
Tel: 61 3 9761 5535 Fax: 61 3 9761 7095

Far East (offices in Singapore, Thailand,
Hong Kong, Taiwan)
Pansing Distribution Pte Ltd
kemal@pansing.com
Tel: 65 6319 9939 Fax: 65 6462 5761

South Africa
Alternative Books
altbook@peterhyde.co.za
Tel: 021 555 4027 Fax: 021 447 1430

Text copyright Nina Power 2009

Design: Stuart Davies

ISBN: 978 1 84694 241 9

A CIP catalogue record for this book is available
from the British Library.

Printed by Digital Book Print

O Books operates a distinctive and ethical publishing philosophy in
all areas of its business, from its global network of authors to
production and worldwide distribution.

CONTENTS

0.0 Introduction

Where have all the interesting women gone? If the contemporary portrayal of womankind were to be believed, contemporary female achievement would culminate in the ownership of expensive handbags, a vibrator, a job, a flat and a man – probably in that order. Of course, no one has to believe the TV shows, the magazines and the adverts, and many don't. But how has it come to this? Did the desires of twentieth-century women's liberation achieve their fulfilment in the shopper's paradise of 'naughty' self-pampering, playboy bunny pendants and bikini waxes? That the height of supposed female emancipation coincides so perfectly with consumerism is a miserable index of a politically desolate time. Much contemporary feminism, however, particularly in its American formulation, doesn't seem too concerned about this coincidence, and this short book is partly an attack on the apparent abdication of any systematic political thought on the part of today's positive, up-beat feminists. It suggests alternative ways of thinking about transformations in work, sexuality and culture that, while seemingly far-fetched in the current ideological climate, may provide more serious material for a feminism of the future.

The book takes its title from Herbert Marcuse's 1964 book *One-Dimensional Man*. In it, Marcuse attempted to analyze the nature and extent of contemporary ideology – the ways in which the modern day subject was not the free and happy individual of capitalist society, but labored instead under the illusory freedoms of technological domination. The 'one-dimensional man' of Marcuse's title is fully immersed in the promissory world of liberal democracy and consumerism and yet 'the spontaneous reproduction of superimposed needs by the individual does not establish autonomy; it only testifies to the efficacy of the controls.'[1] I contend that much of the rhetoric of both consumerism and contemporary feminism is a barrier to any genuine thinking of work, sex and politics that would break with the 'efficacy of the controls' that Marcuse identified. What looks like emancipation is nothing but a tightening of the shackles.

One-Dimensional Woman starts from the premise that we cannot understand anything about what contemporary feminism might be if we neglect to pay attention to specific changes in work and the way in which 'feminism' as a term has come to be used by those who would traditionally have been regarded as the enemies of feminism (see the section 'Hawkish and Mawkish'). The main part of the book deals with changes in work and the so-called 'feminization of labor' – as well as the constant pressure to be self-promoting and available for work. This is of course something that affects men and women alike, but in subtly different ways.

This is not a cheerful book, by any means, but at its heart lies the conviction that women and men have the inherent ability to be something more than one-dimensional. It looks for utopian intimations in alternative histories, particularly in relation to pornography and to various forms of collective and social living. It tries to avoid straightforward assertions of blame – of capitalism, of women themselves, of forms of feminism that do little to address the real questions – because it is never as simple as uncovering a 'better' mode of existence behind the illusion. Such forms of revelation presuppose that the writer is somehow in a privileged position vis-à-vis the dumb, unenlightened masses. People are not stupid, and they know when they are being treated like idiots. It is also clear, unfortunately, that

2

ideology runs deeper than the hopeful might have previously imagined. It is not merely a question of turning the tables or changing the language. As Paolo Virno puts it:

> It would certainly be more comforting to assume that the illusions current today are the product of media propaganda and that they can therefore be refuted by means of a patient pedagogical project of clarification. Unfortunately this is not the case. There is a material basis for ideology, an objective foundation that reinforces and reproduces deception.[2]

This 'objective foundation' is real, and disheartening, but doesn't completely exhaust the field of the possible – there are battles still to be fought, and won. Many of the tactics of feminism thus far – rewriting cultural histories, reclaiming the body, occupying 'male' positions – have had significant effects, but have not been able to touch the basis of the problem at hand. The current 'material basis' of ideology has managed to (temporarily) make classical forms of organization (trade unions, protest groups) seem unnecessary, outmoded and impossible, all at the same time (at least in the more affluent parts of the world). This short book is an attempt to try to identify some of these material obstacles to equality, even – especially – when we're supposed to think that everything is just fine.

0.1 Equality?

Capitalism has had a complex effect on our understanding of 'equality'. On the one hand, there is seemingly nothing discriminatory about the compulsion to accumulate – it doesn't matter who does the work, as long as profit is generated and value extracted. What, then, would be the point of discriminating against women *qua* women? Or blacks *qua* blacks? Or homosexuals *qua* homosexuals? On the other hand, as more or less everybody knows, women still earn less than men for the same work, and are heavily over-represented in part-time and badly-paid jobs, and it is clear that ethnic minorities and homosexuals are massively under-represented in certain forms of employment.

Perhaps, though, we should be less concerned about *representation* than about serious structural and ideological factors. After all, the argument about getting women, ethnic minorities and homosexuals into 'top positions' is an argument that is currently being won by the right. Barack Obama's recent election is perhaps a progressive hint of things to come, but it remains to be seen just how redistributive his 'change' will be. Condoleezza Rice, Ayaan Hirsi Ali and Pim Fortuyn are (or were) all atypical candidates for their respective positions, but it doesn't stop them being, respectively, a war-mongerer, a neo-conservative thinker and an anti-immigration politician who favored a 'cold war' with Islam. All those who (the first election around, anyway) made Margaret Thatcher the first female British Prime Minister 'for feminist reasons' were to be punished for their progressive aspirations with a slew of reforms of a rather different 'progressively' neo-liberal kind. It is not enough to have women in top positions of power, it depends upon what kind of women they are and what they're going to do when they get there. As Lindsey German puts it:

> It is the time of the token woman ... Paradoxically the triumph of the rhetoric of feminism has taken place exactly at a time when the actual conditions of women's lives have worsened, and this rhetoric has been used to justify policies which will harm women.[3]

It has long been clear that we need to extend the concept of tokenism to take account of the fact that often these 'exceptional' women and minorities are not just included in positions of power but come to represent the worst aspects of it. Zillah Eisenstein uses the term 'decoy' to describe the way in which 'imperialist democracy' covers over its structural sins with a thin veneer of representational respectability: 'The manipulation of race and gender as decoys for democracy reveals the corruptibility of identity politics.'[4] Getting women and ethnic minorities into positions of power is not necessarily going to improve the lives of women and ethnic minorities in general, and certainly hasn't so far. Condoleezza Rice may well have been the United States Secretary of State, but it was black women (and black men and children) who suffered most during Hurricane Katrina.[5]

This creates problems for feminism, or at least for an unproblematic usage of the term. The next section shows just how complicated complicated the word can get, via an examination of the phenomenon that was Sarah Palin's 2008 vice-presidential campaign in which 'feminism' came to mean a great many things indeed.

0.2. Sarah Palin, or How Not to be a Feminist

During the build-up to the 2008 American election, Jacques-Alain Miller, arch-Lacanian and part-time moralist, published a piece entitled 'Sarah Palin: Operation "Castration"'.[6] In it, he argued that vice-presidential candidate Palin represents a certain kind of 'post-feminist' woman, one who knows that 'the phallus is a semblance' (more on this anon). Jessica Valenti in *The Guardian* takes the perhaps more intuitive line that Palin is an 'anti-feminist' through and through, because, among other things, she would limit women's right to choose and abolish sex education.[7] Palin herself has long been involved in blurring the boundaries of the term, especially by virtue of her membership of the advocacy organization 'Feminists for Life,' who take an apparently feminist commitment to 'non-aggression' to mean that any violence directed towards a fetus (even if the pregnancy is the result of rape) is incompatible with the supposedly natural non-belligerence of the female sex.

Here we have three different takes on the same word, in which a) for Miller, a pre-Palin feminist would be a woman (Ségolène Royal, for example) who 'imitated man, respected the phallus, and performed as if they had one' and thus would be easy to dismiss as lesser or sub-standard men, b) for Valenti, a feminist is someone who supports a woman's right to choose, who fights for equality in every walk of life and c) for Palin herself, who is both fiercely maternal and politically aggressive, a feminist would indeed be a 'pitbull in lipstick'. A shallow conception of feminism, and a common response whenever individual women achieve power of any substantive kind, would be one that says 'look, there's a woman Prime Minister! A woman CEO! Haven't you gotten what you wanted?' As Valenti puts it, this position is premised on the false belief that that all women want is ... another woman.' Beyond whatever she actually says or does, Palin is painted as a success story for women, simply because she is one.

The Republican abuse of the term feminism in the past decade or so is an astonishing lesson in the politically opportunistic use of language. Where the Right would once have bundled queers, leftists, feminists, peaceniks and other sundry misfits together as internal enemies of the state, when it came to providing reasons for the invasion of Afghanistan, in particular, the language of feminism was suddenly plucked from the dustbin of history as a specifically 'Western' value. 'Respect for women ... can triumph in the Middle East and beyond!' cried Bush in a speech to the UN, perhaps forgetting that on his first day in office he had cut off funding to any international family-planning organizations that offer abortion services or counseling.[8]

It is clear, then, that we are not only dealing with 'right' and 'left' feminism, but with a fundamental crisis in the meaning of the word. If 'feminism' can mean anything from behaving like a man (Miller), being pro-choice (Valenti), being pro-life (Palin), and being pro-war (the Republican administration), then we may simply need to abandon the term, or at the very least, restrict its usage to those situations in which we make quite certain we explain what we mean by it. Valenti opts for a plaintive (if appealing) humanism, with the idea that it's ultimately 'good' or 'bad' people who will win, and that this divide is indifferent to gender: 'the last thing America needs is another corrupt and lying politician – man or woman.'

But the reception of Sarah Palin has not been played out on the grounds of her purported 'feminism' alone. In fact, she has managed to avoid many of the old female dichotomies – mother/politician, attractive/successful, passive/go-getting – by embodying both sides of each all at once at the same time. In this sense, she is the fulfillment of the 1980s imperative that women could (and should) 'have it all' – the babies, the job, the success, the sex. What can't a gun-toting pro-lifer who beats the men on their own turf do? She even trumps many older right-wing women at their own game, those who stand in front of crowds to argue that a woman's place is in the home, staging the spectacle of their own performative contradiction.

As Miller quaintly puts it: 'a Sarah Palin puts forward no lack'. Everything she has in her armory (literally, rhetorically, visually) is in the open. All her potential weaknesses only serve to make her more (super)human, more aggressively populist, more everywoman: the dynamics of her family life, her lack of experience, her hobbies and poses (her love of guns, her 'hockey mom'-ness). Women want to be her,[9] many men (and perhaps even a few women) want to have sex with her (see the Facebook groups: 'I would totally do Sarah Palin', 'Sarah Palin is HOT!' and 'I'd Bang Sarah Palin'). The more interesting of these pro-Palin groups make explicit the link between her attractiveness and the current political spectacle: 'Sarah Palin is stirring things up – and I'm EXCITED' (or, as Miller puts it, in a slightly more literary register: 'she brings a new Eros to politics'). The Facebook group 'Sarah Palin is twice the man Barack will ever be' goes halfway to recognizing her power, but remains trapped within the old idea that to be a woman in politics one must become more like a man.

Miller's argument is not merely that Palin makes a 'better man' than Obama, for example, but that she alone realizes that 'the phallus is only a semblance' – that is, pretending to have power when one does not is not nearly as effective as understanding the contingent nature of the field of power (or meaning) and exploiting it at every turn. Palin is not pretending to be a man – she is pretending to be all women at once, and yet perfectly mundane. The Facebook group 'I Am Terrified of Sarah Palin' perhaps captures some of Miller's fear: 'For the moment, a woman who plays the "castration" card is invincible.' For Miller, Palin's ability to castrate – to invoke the fear of emasculation by undermining the very symbolic register in which castration anxiety can be warded off – is literally petrifying: 'they [her political opponents, her media enemies] have no idea how to attack a woman who uses her femininity to ridicule them.'

The anxiety that a figure like Sarah Palin induces is not the old one of noting with horror the lack ('why don't girls have what I have?'), but of the greater fear of a vast female plenitude. America has found its new hero(ine), and she's a woman who turns the insults that every successful woman has hurled at her (dog, bitch, flirt) into ammunition to shoot dead her accusers. She turns maternity into a war-weapon, inexperience into a populist virtue and feminism into something that even the Christian Right could approve of.

Although Palin didn't manage to make Vice President this time around, what she represents – a kind of terminator hockey-mom who calls herself a feminist – is something quite new, and relates to a broader change in the recent fortunes of the term. The rise of the pro-war 'feminist' and the rhetoric of female emancipation in the cause of belligerent foreign policy is worth exploring in more detail.

0.3 Hawkish and Mawkish

One of the more profound and disturbing recent shifts in geopolitical discourse is the co-opting of the language of feminism by figures who ten or fifteen years ago would have spoken out most vociferously against what feminism stands for. The invasions of Afghanistan and Iraq were both justified by an appeal to the emancipation of women, and the discourse of feminism was specifically invoked. George W. Bush's wife, Laura, prepared the ground with a radio broadcast that declared that 'only the terrorists and the Taliban threaten to pull out women's fingernails for wearing nail polish.'[10] The battle for public support for the wars was played out through a combination of the liberal 'feminist' discourse of rights and the hawkish premise that only carpet-bombing the oppressive enemy could solve the problem. Just as the Bush administration neglected to ask their experienced diplomats about others ways in which geopolitics could be discussed, they neglected to work with grassroots feminists at work in Afghanistan and Iraq. As Katha Pollitt puts it:

> US invasions have made the work of Muslim feminists much more difficult. The last thing they need is for women's rights to be branded as the tool of the invaders and occupiers and cultural imperialists.[11]

Bombing in the name of women's rights assumes that all women, particularly Muslim women, are straightforwardly victims in need of a gruff, vicious dragging out of the mire by forces who know better. Closer to home, it is clear that the rhetoric of hawkish feminism remains just that – as the Bush administration ploughs yet more money into useless abstinence programs and the restrictions on abortion become ever tighter. Feminism is something merely to invoke to convince fence-sitting morally-minded voters that war is the only option on the table.

As a political term, 'feminism' has become so broad that it can be used to justify almost anything, even the invasion of other countries. As Katherine Viner puts it:

> Feminism is used for everything these days, except the fight for true equality – to sell trainers, to justify body mutilations, to make women make porn, to help men get off rape charges, to ensure women feel they have self-respect because they use a self-esteem-enhancing brand of shampoo. No wonder it's being used as a reason for bombing women and children too.[12]

But how has this happened? Viner points out that the rhetoric of feminism in the name of war is not as new as it might seem:

> ...this theft of feminist rhetoric is not new, particularly if its function is national expansion; in fact, it has a startling parallel with another generation of men who similarly cared little for the liberation of women. The Victorian male estab-lishment, which led the great imperialistic ventures of the 19th century, fought bitterly against women's increasingly vocal feminist demands and occasional successes (a handful going to university; new laws permitting married women to own property); but at the same time, across the globe, they used the language of feminism to acquire the booty of the colonies.[13]

Clearly if something is to be salvaged of the 'fight for true equality', the meaning of feminism must be clear. It must also recognize the way in which it has been colonized not only by warmongers, but also by consumerism and contemporary ideologies of work. It is not inconceivable that there will come a time in which women will no longer say 'I'm not a feminist' because they're worried about putting men off, but because they don't want to associated with its invocation by the bellicose.

In this sense then, rather than retaining the idea of feminism as something that stretched from its radical incarnation to its liberal form, we have to broaden the scope of its reference to the whole of the political spectrum. Imperialist feminism uses the language of liberal feminism (extending human rights, extending the vote) but the techniques of war. It is invariably counter-productive, and in its current phase primarily anti-Islamic. The devout Islamic woman becomes the antithesis of a certain kind of strident right-wing feminist. Alain Badiou has identified the contradictory imperatives behind the recent anti-headscarf laws in France as an example of this logic:

Grandiose causes need new-style arguments. For example: hijab must be banned; it is a sign of male power (the father or eldest brother) over young girls or women. So, we'll banish the women who obstinately wear it. Basically put: these girls or women are oppressed. Hence, they shall be punished. It's a little like saying: 'This woman has been raped: throw her in jail.'... Or, contrariwise: it is they who freely want to wear that damned headscarf, those rebels, those brats! Hence, they shall be punished. Wait a minute: do you mean it isn't the symbol of male oppression, after all? The father and eldest brother have nothing to do with it? Where then does the need to ban the scarf come from? The problem with hijab is that it is conspicuously religious. Those brats have made their belief conspicuous. You there! Go stand in the corner![14]

On the one hand, any woman who wears the hijab must, by the logic of secular reason, be oppressed. On the other, if she makes too much of the rhetoric of choice to justify her wearing it, she misunderstands precisely what that rhetoric is for. The logic of choice, of the market, of the right to pick between competing products cannot be used to justify the decision to wear what one likes, if one chooses something that indicates a desire to not play the game. But which game? This double-logic of the anger against the headscarf is exemplified in the following excruciating complaint by David Aaronovitch from 2003:

> My greatest feelings of discomfort, however, are reserved for those religious people who are obviously and outwardly pious. Because here I really do not know what is being demanded of me. Take the hijab – the headscarf worn by many Muslim women – a rarity 20 years ago, but now ubiquitous in many big cities. Is it saying, 'Don't look at me', or 'Look at me'?[15]

This idea that something is being 'demanded' of him is bizarre, but perhaps can be understood according to the logic of deeper circuits of desire. From the same Badiou piece:

> Strange is the rage reserved by so many feminist ladies for the few girls wearing the hijab. They have begged poor president Chirac... to crack down on them in the name of the Law. Meanwhile the prostituted female body is everywhere. The most humiliating pornography is universally sold. Advice on sexually exposing bodies lavishes teen magazines day in and day out.
>
> A single explanation: a girl must show what she's got to sell. She's got to show her goods. She's got to indicate that, henceforth, the circulation of women abides by the gener-alized model, and not by restricted exchange. Too bad for

bearded fathers and elder brothers! Long live the planetary market! The generalized model is the top fashion model.

It used to be taken for granted that an intangible female right is to only have to get undressed in front of the person of her choosing. But no. It is vital to hint at undressing at every instant. Whoever covers up what she puts on the market is not a loyal merchant.

Let's argue the following, then, a pretty strange point: the law on the hijab is a pure capitalist law. It orders femininity to be exposed. In other words, having the female body circulate according to the market paradigm is obligatory. For teenagers, i.e. the teeming center of the entire subjective universe, the law bans any holding back.[16]

The imperative for girls to show what they have to sell, to 'hint at undressing', to have the female body circulate as part of a strategy of employability and consumerism renders the hijab an object of angry, law-obsessed confusion. Aaronovitch's uncertainty about whether it means 'Don't look at me', or 'Look at me' is interpretable solely in terms of a generalized imperative that all femininity be translatable into the logic of the market. If the body is a useful part of the 'package', then all the better. Men too are increasingly prey to this imperative, to be an all-round self-seller, but it is in this heavily politicized continuum from (bad) hijab-wearer to (good) proto-porn actress that the contemporary ideology of work is most clearly seen – and it is primarily played out in the circulation of female bodies.

1.0 The Feminization of Labor

> However terrible and disgusting the dissolution of the old
> family ties within the capitalist system may appear, large scale
> industry, by assigning an important part in socially organized
> processes of production, outside the sphere of the domestic
> economy, to women, young persons and children of both sexes,
> does nevertheless create a new economic foundation for a
> higher form of the family and of relations between the sexes.
>
> – Karl Marx[17]

No discussion of the current fortunes of women can take place
outside of a discussion of work. The inclusion of women into the
labor force has brought about unprecedented changes in the way
we understand the 'role' of women, the capacity of women to live
independent lives and the way in which women participate in
the economy more generally. Of course, women have always
worked, that is to say, raised children, tended to the home, grown
crops, etc., and how different the history of the world would
have been had this been from the start been regarded as labor to
be rewarded. Nevertheless, as Marx notes, it is only when
women enter work 'outside the sphere of the domestic economy'
that transformations in relations between the sexes, the compo-
sition of families and so on, really start to happen. The ability to
be 'flexible' that all good pre-workers now imbibe with their
mother's milk is the admission that there is no natural role for
women to occupy and that, at least at the beginning of one's

working life, no job is out of bounds. From the perky A level photos that beam out from August newspapers, to the successful young professional featured on the advertisement for a new luxury flat development, the job market seems, at least on the surface, a better place to be for women than men.

On the whole, women have adapted remarkably well to work. They now do better at school, better at university, and go to work before, during and after pregnancy. They have been 'encouraged' by a government desperate to get mothers, in particular, back to work, even without providing adequate access to child care. In the UK, unlike many other European countries, female participation in the labor market has been high for a long time, and women, particularly young, single women, are a key factor in the proliferation and success of job agencies, turning precarity into a virtue. One does not need to be an essentialist about traditionally 'female' traits (for example, loquacity, caring, relationality, empathy) to think that there is something notable going on here: women are encouraged to regard themselves as good communicators, the kind of person who'd be 'ideal' for agency or call-centre work. The professional woman needs no specific skills as she is *simply* professional, that is to say, perfect for the kind of work that deals with communication in its purest sense.

There is a curiously existential aspect to this now intimate link between women and labor. Male and female graduates have somewhat different attitudes to work, according to one 2006 study:

It would seem some men and some women graduates are approaching job seeking rather differently, particularly when they are having trouble finding work straight away. The women's view is, 'My dream job hasn't arrived, so I will go out and get a few more skills and more experience under my belt so that when it arrives I will be ready'. Men are perhaps thinking, 'My dream job hasn't arrived yet – I will just stay here until it does.'[18]

Female pragmatism, the supposed sensibleness of women, finds itself translated neatly into the language of skill-acquisition and self-advancement.

Fewer women than men currently claim Jobseekers Allowance, and there are many more women in part-time work (1.80 million men to 5.70 million women as of mid-2008).[19] Employment agencies often have girly names and pink-tinged logos, like 'Office Angels' and 'Capability Jane', enticing young women into secretarial work that will be extremely unlikely to last more than 13 weeks at any given location (at which point the employer would be legally obliged to give the worker some paid time off). Agency work is sold as a type of liberation, the good kind of 'flexibility', with the added advantage for the agency and the firm that the worker will never know who her 'colleagues' are. Organizing among agency workers is structurally impossible, and the enforced atomization of the agency worker is rephrased as 'individual choice', 'your freedom'. This maneuver crops up time and time again. At the very moment where some sort of collective response might be appropriate – for example, campaigning against discrimination of pregnant women at work – the language of choice is invoked: 'it was her *choice* to get pregnant, why should we have to work more to cover her time off?' Childless women are pitted against those with families, the young against the older. A recent report claimed that '76% of managers admitted that they would not hire a new recruit if they knew they were going to fall pregnant within six months of starting the job.'[20] Obviously women are still expected to carry the majority of the burden of childcare, regardless of whether the fathers want to be involved, and this conflicts with their roles as enthusiastic and fully-available workers. When women confront the blank white wall of motherhood, which most definitely curtails their 'flexibility' in more ways than one, the boss can shrug his or her hands and say 'look, you're not what you said you were. Sorry!' Any general social responsibility for motherhood, or move towards the equal sharing of childcare responsibilities is immediately blocked off – this individual woman has betrayed the economy! All the while, women working full time receive 17% less than male counterparts while part-timers are paid on average 37% less.[21] The model female worker, so long as she doesn't get pregnant or make undue demands, is both desirable and cheap.

When people talk about the 'feminization of labor', then, their discourse is often double-edged. The phrase is at once descriptive (work is generally more precarious and communication-based, as women's jobs tended to be in the past) and an expression of resentment ('women have stolen proper men's jobs! It's their fault - somehow - that we don't have any proper industry anymore!'). There are more women in work, and work itself has become more 'female'. As Cristina Morini puts it, the feminization of labor 'is used to define not only the objective aspect of the quantitative increase in the active female population, around the world, but increasingly underlines the qualitative and constituent character of this phenomenon.'[22] Alternatively, we could turn this around and talk about the laborization of women – the way in which females are cast as worker first and only secondarily as mother or wife, or any other identity position not linked with economic productivity. Obviously neither the feminization of labor nor the laborization of women are total phenomena, nor complete. The glorious world of work stumbles at various obstacles: pregnancy, age, lack of education, desperation (particularly of migrant and illegal workers, the nannies and cleaners who work so that richer women can do the same). The job market continues to differentiate between men and women – the most blatant is the surprisingly resilient pay differential for the same jobs, and the predominance of women in part-time and badly-paid work. Sometimes this is related to an underlying assumption about who bears the brunt of the burden for childcare, but not always. If men's wages too have been depressed, if there literally aren't enough jobs, or enough money to pay for them (what with the dire need to pay CEOs so many more times more than anyone else, not to mention the precious shareholders), then the category 'woman' remains a useful one for the 'first fired, last hired' policy that has characterized the employment market for much of the last hundred years or so. The discourse of work as pure emancipation depends on blocking out class and age constantly. The menopausal unconscious comes back to haunt the perky young professional; the specter of the ex-worker at home looking after her kids angers the market even as it depends on biological reproduction to sustain its own future.

Nevertheless, images of a certain kind of successful woman proliferate – the city worker in heels, the flexible agency employee, the hard-working hedonist who can afford to spend her income on vibrators and wine – and would have us believe that – yes – capitalism is a girl's best friend. The demand to be a 'adaptable' worker, to be constantly 'networking', 'selling yourself', in effect, to become a kind of walking CV is felt keenly by both sexes in the developed world. Arguably, however, this omnipresent imperative is interpreted differently by the sexes. David Harvey poses this question in the following way: 'what effect does the circulation of variable capital (the extraction of labor power and surplus value) have on the bodies (persons and subjectivities) of those through whom it circulates?'[23] If the contemporary world of work on one level doesn't care who does the job as long as it is done, on the other it cannot forget the internal history of the transformations in gender roles when it has costs to shave or profits to reap by doing so – capitalism selectively remembers that women are women. Morini argues that transformations in the organization of work, particularly the rise of precarity, means that labor itself has become essentially feminized:

Work is an effective occasion for the emancipation of women in the face of male oppression, albeit within the limits set by the hierarchical organization of work. Thanks to the level of generalized precariousness, which has been transformed into a structural element of contemporary capitalism, 'work which becomes a woman', is tantamount to saying that the fragmentation of the service provided and the complexity of the dependence/absorption which women have experienced at various times in the labor market, ends up becoming a general paradigm irrespective of gender. In this sense, it can be maintained that the figure of social precariousness today is woman: in cognitive capitalism precariousness, mobility and fragmentation become constituent elements of the work of all persons irrespective of gender.[24]

All work has become women's work, even that of men. No wonder the young professional woman beams down at us from real estate billboards as the paradigmatic image of achievement. As Virno puts it 'correctly understood, post-Fordist "profession-ality" does not correspond to any precise profession. It consists rather of certain character traits.'[25] At this point in economic time, those character traits are remarkably feminine, which is why the pragmatic, enthusiastic professional woman is the symbol for the world of work as a whole.

1.1 You're Like an Advert for Yourself

This feminization of labor is also a feminization of the search for labor. If men and women are at all times supposed to be a kind of walking CV, constantly networking, constantly advertising themselves, then this 'body' is the prime locus for any understanding of the way in which the logic of employment overcodes our very comportment. From the top to the bottom of the employment pool, whether one is a jobseeker being retrained for work or a CEO manipulating contacts, your bodily existence at work comes to coincide with the CV that neatly summarizes where you've been and how you made profitable use of your time. Even those at the very bottom of the rung – migrant laborers hired to perform a particular menial task, say, must demonstrate their willingness to work, to 'sell themselves', all the more so if a large army of reserve labor is waiting to take your place.

Clearly, anything you have on your side, whether you've worked/studied/paid for it or not, is part of your job-seeking arsenal. Far from being something to keep in reserve, or relevant only to those on close terms, one's looks, manner and appearance are all. This is not simply a matter of 'looking smart' for work, but rather a matter of being in a position where everything counts, up to and including one's most basic subjective and physical attitudes. Everything is on show, everything counts.

From the boardroom to the strip-club, one must capitalize on one's assets at every moment, demonstrating that one is indeed a good worker, a motivated employee, and that nothing prevents your full immersion in the glorious world of work.

If we accept the argument that the division between 'free-time' and 'labor time' has become extremely blurred in recent years, there is something potentially revealing about what individuals choose to do in their 'spare time', especially in moments of 'extreme' leisure such as the American tradition of Spring Break, a kind of beach-based sex 'n' booze free-for-all, documented from time to time by the 'Girls Gone Wild' franchise, whose basic modus operandi is to visit college towns, filming girls in stages of drunkenness and clothelessness. When the 'Girls Gone Wild' team hand out hats or t-shirts in exchange for a shot of breasts, or the performance of a snog with another woman, the logic is right out in the open: we'll give you something obviously crap in exchange for a kind of performance that reveals that there is nothing subjective, nothing left, hidden behind the appearance, that you simply are commensurate with your comportment in the world. You are your breasts.

All of this marks a very serious transformation in the relationship between women and their bodies. Far from flaunting their assets in the hope that the refracted attention will filter back to their person as a whole (in Sartre's example of *mauvaise foi*, a young woman out on a date treats her hand as a dead object when it is reached for by her lascivious beau, and speaks instead of 'elevated' matters in order to temporarily and deliciously suspend what she knows to be true – that the young man desires her sexually), it is the 'assets', the parts, that take on the function of the whole. The all-pervasive peepshow segmentarity of contemporary culture demands that women treat their breasts as *wholly separate entities*, with little or no connection to themselves, their personality, or even the rest of their body. All autonomous, organic agency of a moral, rational or egoic nature is dissolved into auto-objectivization.

They, the breasts, and not their 'owner', are the centre of attention, and are referred to, with alarming regularity, as completely autonomous objects, much as one would refer to suitcases or doughnuts. Constantly fiddled with, adjusted, exposed, covered-up or discussed, contemporary breasts resemble nothing so much as bourgeois pets: idiotic, toothless, yapping dogs with ribbons in their hair and personalized carrying pouches. These milkless objects of bemused scopophilia (frequently and explicitly 'fake', as is the fashion) are described over and over as if possessed of their own will and desire, separate from that of their owners ('Oh no! It slipped out of my top! Again!'). It is as if plastic surgery and the concomitant bloodletting did not expunge a malevolent spirit, but insert one. The thing to say upon first glance is no longer 'you look nice' but 'are those real?' A. A. Gill writing of Abby Titmuss, puts it thus: '[she] speaks of her breasts' inability to remain covered, as if they were a medical condition she had to live with, with as much good humor, and stoicism as she could muster. The outbreaks of exhibitionist sexuality were like eczema attacks: disgusting, unsightly but not her fault.'[26] The jokey male hypothetical question to lesbians ('don't you spend all day playing with your breasts?') has literally come true. They are 'assets' in the physical and economic senses simultaneously and as much use as possible is to be extracted from them – their role in breastfeeding is perversely secondary to their primary function as secondary sexual characteristics.

What the autonomous breasts and the concomitant becoming-CV of the human means is that the language of objectification may not be useful any longer, as there is no (or virtually no) subjective dimension left to be colonized. The language of objectification demands on a minimal subjective difference, what Badiou quaintly identified in the realm of personal relations as 'the intangible female right ... to only have to get undressed in front of the person of her choosing.' In the realm of work we could call this the right not to have to lay bare one's entire personality and private life. In effect, this is what the world of work increasingly demands – that one is always contactable (by email, by phone), that one is always an 'ambassador' for the firm (don't write anything about your job on your blog), that there is no longer any separation between the private realm and the working day (Facebook amalgamates friends and colleagues alike). The personal is no longer just political, it's economic through and through.

Perhaps a further sign of the death of the objective/subjective opposition comes in the form of a parodic historical inversion. It's relatively acceptable for women to make general (usually whiny) claims about men, or to say that a man has a 'cute arse', even at work, because it's so obviously a toothless parody of the sexism of decades past. Objectification implies that there is something left over in the subject that resists such a capture, that we might protest if we thought someone was trying to deny such interiority, but it's not clear that contemporary work allows anyone to have an inner life in the way we might once have understood it.

The blurring of work, social, personal and physical life is almost total. If feminism is to have a future, it has to recognize the new ways in which life and existence are colonized by new forms of domination that go far beyond objectification as it used to be understood.

2.0 Consumer Feminism

I did this interview where I just mentioned that I read Foucault.
Who doesn't in university, right! I was in this strip club giving
this guy a lap dance and all he wanted to do was to discuss
Foucault with me. Well I can stand naked and do my little
dance, or I can discuss Foucault, but not at the same time.

– Annabel Chong, 1999

Contemporary feminism has attempted to provide answers to a
wide range of questions – work, sex, porn, family. And if we take
the answers at face value, the future looks bright! Books like
Manifesta: Young Women, Feminism and the Future and *Full-Frontal
Feminism* aim to capture the youth feminist market with
seemingly endless amounts of 'sass' and breathless confidence-
building. It's a strange but relatively successful form of self-help,
which takes its cue from books like Gloria Steinem's 1992
Revolution from Within: A Book of Self-Esteem. In these books, the
political and historical dimensions of feminism are subsumed
under the imperative to feel better about oneself, to become a
more robust individual. As a response to the 'I'm not a feminist,
but…' pose it's very successful. Almost everything turns out to be
'feminist' – shopping, pole-dancing, even eating chocolate. This
section attempts to demonstrate the remarkable similarity
between 'liberating' feminism and 'liberating' capitalism, and the
way in which the desire for emancipation starts to look like
something wholly interchangeable with the desire simply to buy

more things. These themes are examined through a brief tour of the key markers of contemporary femininity – cinema, magazines, self-harm, chocolate, and a strange kind of theological romanticism...

2.1 Feminism™: Two Sides of the Same Con

Feminism offers you the latest deals in lifestyle improvement, from the bedroom to the boardroom, from guilt-free fucking to the innocent hop-skip all the way to the shopping mall – I don't diet so it's ok! *I'm* not deluded! I can buy what I like! Feminism™ is the perfect accompaniment to femme-capital™: Politics, such as it is, belongs to the well-balanced individual (the happy shopper), sassiness is like, *so* where it's at (consumer confidence) and, most of all, one must never, *ever* admit to cracks in the facade (ideology). This foundation is flawless! And it lasts all night! Unlike *men*, titter, titter, etc. etc.

A recent puff piece for equality by Jessica Valenti informs us that not only does feminism do wonders for one's flat ('as I was getting ready for the photoshoot for this article, the guy I'm dating ... tidied up for me so the photographer wouldn't see what a tip my apartment is at the weekends'), it actually makes life more *fun*. You see, girls, it's not all about grim-faced non-shaving and being a bit angry. Feminism can, like, totally help you out. Take Valenti's job description, for instance:

> I have an amazing group of women friends who spend their days speaking out against sexist idiocy – and who also happily dance their asses off with me when we're out clubbing.[27]

Apart from the rhetorical horror of folk actually 'dancing their asses off', Valenti's argument is a desperate bid to sell feminism as the latest must-have accessory. Trotting out the tired old line 'I used to think that all feminists were miserable and hairy', Valenti does her very best to sell us her feminist manifesto, in all its faux-radicality: 'liking your body can be a revolutionary act' she concludes, regarding her navel with a curious kind of joy as centuries of political movements that dared to regard the *holy body* as secondary to egalitarian and impersonal projects crumble to bits around her. Incidentally, for the disproportionate fear that the statistically and historically minimal group of women who were both angry *and* had hairy legs have inculcated both in their detractors and in their wannabe-successors, we should salute them as often as possible.

Stripped of any internationalist and political quality, feminism becomes about as radical as a diamanté phone cover. Valenti 'truly believes' that feminism is necessary for women 'to live happy, fulfilled lives'. Slipping down as easily as a friendly-bacteria yoghurt drink, Valenti's version of feminism, with its total lack of structural analysis, genuine outrage or collective demand, believes it has to compliment capitalism in order to effectively sell its product. When she claims that 'ladies, we have to take individual action', what she really means is that it's every woman for herself, and if it is the Feminist™ woman who gets the nicest shoes and the chocolatiest sex, then that's just too bad for you, sister.

To Freud's infamous question, 'what do women want?' it seems, then, that we have all-too-ready an answer. Why! They want shoes and chocolate and handbags and babies and curling tongs washed down with a large glass of white wine and a complaint about their job/men/friends (delete as appropriate). This model of contemporary womanhood, as specific to advanced industrialized countries as it is, is everywhere.

It is not enough to say that women are being sold a lie by

advertising, magazines and cinema. People have been saying this for decades. Debates about whether thin models 'cause' anorexia, or whether standards of beauty contribute to rising levels of depression, self-harm and anxiety are never quite satisfactory, even if there must be some truth to them.

What is striking about *Elle, Vogue*, etc., apart from the relentlessly contentless writing, was just how *confusing* they are. Far from whacking you over the head with some specific set of physical ambitions, they create a far more complex set of anxieties and conflicting demands. Take the 15 pages or so of 'this season's fashions'– if you were to 'follow' all of the trends equally, you'd be a corporate-goth-bohemian-neon-native-American-Indian-casual-office girl. Which would probably look *quite interesting*, but I doubt that's what they mean. But there is literally no way of distinguishing *between* fashions – assuming one cared about such things, you'd probably want to know which one was *more* fashionable. Only the very rich could afford to follow them all.

The same goes for the models – certainly, the one thing they do have in common is thinness, that weird kind where it looks like your limbs are on backwards – but how different they all look, and yet how strangely they all look like a foodstuff. Photoshop has turned fashion photography into something you'd want to lick, rather than emulate. And the whole libidinal economy of half-naked women staring up at you, as if you were the owner of a peculiarly classical male gaze. It's not clear whether you are supposed to envy or admire them – but then, that's not clear in the real world either. Clearly 'not knowing which' (model to look like, fashion to pick) is a brilliant way of creating just the right kind of anxiety appropriate to a form of shopping frenzy that will buy as many and as varied kinds of shoes, etc., in order to get as close as possible to this set of incoherent demands. For fashion to survive the one thing the magazines and adverts can never say, of course, is: 'work out what suits you and stick to that!'. Fashion magazines are most definitely tied up with impossible demands, but they seem far more comprehensible as motors of economic expenditure than as ego-ideals.

But if fashion is more usefully run as a confusing anxiety-inducing operation, the presentation of sex – both the emancipatory 'feminist' kind and the capitalist ad-selling kind – is remarkably homogeneous. Ariel Levy in *Female Chauvinist Pigs* has gone some way in describing this culture:

> A tawdry, tarty, cartoonlike version of female sexuality has become so ubiquitous, it no longer seems particular. What we once regarded as a *kind* of sexual expression we now view *as* sexuality.[28]

This is clearly not the liberation once imagined – think of Germaine Greer's handwringing over her calls to emancipate female sexuality coming 'true' but ultimately ending up as 'slut' t-shirts for pre-teens. Capitalism, which in a sense knows no morals (or at least can change them easily), couldn't care less about the positive, happy, 'feminist' reclaiming of sex so long as it makes a buck out of skimpy nightwear and thongs. Levy's concept of 'female chauvinist pigs', 'women who make sex objects of other women and of themselves', is perhaps not so new as all that – after all, women's magazines that invite you to condemn and envy other women in equal measures have been around for a long time – but Levy is right that this has taken on a peculiarly pornographic taint in recent years.

There are many who regard the sexualized treatment of women by other women with an understandable kind of feminist-humanist horror: women can't possibly treat other women the way we said unenlightened men do! But they can, and they do. Sometimes this sexualization is done directly – take, for example, the vexed role of the performance of lesbianism to titillate straight male friends. Clearly there is nothing inherently nicer about women than men. Levy ultimately falls into the trap of opposing a nice, liberated version of sexuality – 'we need to allow ourselves the freedom to figure out what we internally want from sex'[29] – to a plastic, cartoon world of breast implants and pole-dancing. There is nothing wrong with Levy's position, in fact, it is extremely sympathetic. But there is problem if there is no way back to this 'freedom' to explore some supposed 'real' sexuality. What if the self-commodification of individuals is all-encompassing, as the analysis of the job-market suggests? What if there is no longer a gap between an internal realm of desires, wants and fantasies and the external presentation of oneself as a sexual being? If the image is the reality? As depressing as this might be, it would make a more useful starting point than to assume there is a real humanist reserve of nice sexual desire lying beneath all the images. If indeed there are moments of subjective resistance, they might not be particularly pleasant. Take self-harm or 'cutting', for example, particularly common among women. What we are dealing with is an attempt to induce reality, to create a feeling of reality. If the red stuff flows, it is an indication that all is not yet lost in what remains of the 'private sphere', that some 'little things' resist capture. (Tattoos, on the other hand, for all their counter-cultural history ultimately indicate some sort of acceptance of the realm of conditioned meaning.) All that can be said for the private tribes of (mostly) women cutters is that they do not understand each other symbol-ically, that there is no communication across scars. Self-harm as the anti-tattoo. Each individualized real-time concentrated creation of reality is the true point of the pain, not the residual scratches (however deep) that remain. Christina Ricci speaks about her own experience of cutting her arms with nails and the tops of fizzy-drinks cans: 'it's a sort of experiment, to see if I can handle pain…it's like having a drink but quicker.' *It's like having a drink but quicker*, an instantaneous chemical smack to the back of the head to calm you down.

So conditioned are we to think that our behaviors are individual (a degree is an 'investment', starting a family is a 'personal choice'), that we miss the collective and historical dimensions of our current situation. Currently, women are 'doing well' and make 'good workers'. The idea that women are the 'sensible' ones, as opposed to bohemian, imaginative men has a history, and it's quite a strange one. The 'genius' typically possesses feminine characteristics – imagination, intuition, emotion, madness – but is not of course an actual woman: the great artist is a *feminine* male, but not a feminine female or a masculine female. Women can be mad, but not aesthetically inspired, or they can be sane, and provide comfort for the true creators, who are a little bit womanish, but not too much.

But are women *really* more sensible? It's unlikely that women are inherently more stable than men, and historically at various points they definitely weren't *supposed* to be (consider the 'hysterical' woman of the 19th century, the Soviet divorce and abortion laws of 1917-18 that recognized that women were just as uncommitted to the bourgeois family set-up as men, Friedan's 'the problem with no name' of the 1950s and 60s). Sometimes women are supposed to be demented harpies with wombs full of devils and other times they're supposed to fold up nicely like the ironing board in a suburban bungalow.

There's been a trope for a while among male blog writers, for example, to refer to their other halves in passing as *her indoors* – the women who supposedly disapprove of their silly male obsessions with record collecting, who drag the boys away from playing with their toys and make them do 'family things' instead. It seems disingenuous, a kind of cover story to mask the fact that, among other things, they might actually enjoy playing with their kids or hanging out with their partner. It also subtly perpetuates the idea that it's men who really have obsessions, even if they mock themselves a bit about it. It's like a safety net – you can like the most avant-garde music/films/literature, but go home to a perfectly normal little family with all its little sexual edicts and dull domesticities. Men have ideas and arguments and fixations, women are balanced and well-rounded. Because women are so much more *worldly*, aren't they? They just know how things work. *'Cup of tea, love?'*

Certainly, there is this prevalent image of the successful, sorted young woman with enough enthusiasm and emotional reserves after passing all those A levels to look after a fragile, tortured young man. But really, women no more know what's going on than men do, and they certainly don't have a insight into nice, stable normality (as if anyone does). The current sorted young woman *imago* is rather conveniently the sort of worker best suited for the type of jobs on offer, but it doesn't mean that in a few years time women won't go back to being depicted as deranged Jezebels hell-bent on fucking society up with their roaming womb-induced crazy-thoughts.

One of the problems with the kind of up-beat jolly feminism presented by Valenti et al. is that it brooks no failure. Take some of the following lines from *Full Frontal Feminism*: 'When you're a feminist, day-to-day life is better. You make better decisions. You have better sex.'[30] and 'Is there anything wrong with being ugly, fat, or hairy? Of course not. But let's be honest: No one wants to be associated with something that is seen as uncool and unattractive. But the thing is, feminists are pretty cool (and attractive!) women.'[31] Furthermore, 'feminism is something you define for yourself.'[32] If feminism is something you define for yourself, then what's to stop it being pure egotism, pure naked greed? Absolutely nothing. 'Feminism says that you have a right to enjoy yourself. An obligation, even.'[33] An obligation to enjoy oneself? Few things are more menacing. According to Valenti, masturbation 'even motivates you to buy fun vibrators that are neon or shaped like rabbits.'[34] Masturbation is a pre-condition for shopping? Feminism simply *is* one's purchasing power:

We may not be able to escape the porn/pop culture ridiculousness, but we can try to use it to create a more reality-based sexuality for ourselves.[35]

It's a nice thought, but the chances of it succeeding are about as likely as Barbie growing a beard.

But a hip young feminist must have her indulgences. Just as pink has become the color that somehow symbolizes both freedom and sexual availability, like a curious form of hygienic nakedness (think of Hugh Hefner's claim that 'the *Playboy* girl has no lace, no underwear, she is naked, well-washed with soap and water, and she is happy'[36]), chocolate has come to indicate that its female devourer is a little bit, well, 'naughty'.

Take, for example, the Iranian business woman, Anousheh Ansari, who paid to go into space:

> Ansari said to ABC News that she didn't care what was on the menu on the International Space Station as long as there was one thing – chocolate.[37]

You've paid twenty million dollars to go into space, and all you can think about is *chocolate*? All humanity's technological and mathematical capacities stretched to breaking-point in the name of the abstract, pointless beauty of extra-terrestrial exploration, and yet a Flake in front of the telly might have done?

Chocolate represents that acceptable everyday extravagance that all-too-neatly encapsulates just the right kind of perky passivity that feminized capitalism just loves to reward with a bubble bath and some crumbly cocoa solids. It sticks in the mouth a bit. In a total abnegation of her own subjective capacity as well as the entire history of human achievement, Fay Weldon, for example, claims that:

> What makes women happy? Ask them and they'll reply, in

roughly this order: sex, food, friends, family, shopping, chocolate.

I think there's a very real sense in which woman are supposed to say 'chocolate' whenever someone asks them what they want. It irresistibly symbolizes any or all of the following: ontological girlishness, a naughty virginity that gets its kicks only from a widely-available mucky cloying substitute, a kind of pecuniary decadence.

This is very much in keeping with the flip-side to the young feminism of Valenti and co, which is the depressed, weird world of Fay Weldon, once a strange misanthropic writer with interesting female characters, now reduced to suggesting that for a happy life women should fake orgasms and follow these rules:

>...sit quietly and smile. Never when in the company of the man you're after do you give him a hard time. You never argue, quarrel, demand your rights, reproach or give him one iota of emotional, intellectual or physical discomfort.[38]

Because what 'men' and indeed, other women, really need is *more* passive, silent, dull, faux-pleasant girls. It is hard to decide which of the sexes Weldon is actually more insulting to here. Men she portrays as too stupid to see through bad porn acting while spending the rest of the time apparently thinking 'solely about pleasure and completion'. Women, on the other hand, are stunted, physically limited creatures who garner pathetic slips of happiness from chocolate and shoes and never come. But where do we get these ideas from? Cinema and television just might have something to do with it...

2.2 Consumer Culture: Girls on Film

What does contemporary visual culture say about women? Here a thought experiment comes in handy: The so-called 'Bechdel Test', first described in Alison Bechdel's comic strip *Dykes to Watch Out For*, consists of the following rules, to be applied to films, but could easily be extended to literature:

1. Does it have at least two women in it,
2. Who [at some point] talk to each other,
3. About something besides a man.

Writer Charles Stross adds that

> if you extend #3 only slightly, to read 'About something besides men or marriage or babies', you can strike out about 50% of the small proportion of mass-entertainment movies that do otherwise seem to pass the test.[39]

Once you know about the test, it's impossible not to apply it, however casually. Stross is right – huge quantities of cultural output (possibly even more than he suggests) fail. Several questions emerge from the test:

1. What is so frightening about women talking to each other without the mediation of their supposed interest in men/marriage/babies?

2. Does cinema/literature have a duty to representation such that it is duty bound to include such scenes, as opposed to pursuing its own set of agendas? Why should literature/cinema be 'realistic' when it could be whatever it wants to be?
3. Does reality *itself* pass the test? How much of the time? Can we 'blame' films/TV for that?

Vera Chytilová's *Daisies* is one of the few films that basically passes the test throughout, and it's clear that it disturbs as much as it charms. This 1966 Czech film features two young women who dedicate their lives to spoiling everything in increasingly surreal ways, with seemingly little rhyme or reason. Who are these irresponsible young women who find it more amusing to play with each other, and occasionally with men, but only so they can return to each other and be yet more 'spoiled' (as in ruined, rather than pampered, of course)? The formal inventiveness of the film would undermine its claims to 'realism', but this is all the better. For all the male 'coming of age' stories in the world, it makes sense that their rare female equivalent would have to be as bizarre as possible. Contemporary mainstream cinema seems, on the whole, retrograde compared to its earlier incarnations, as if a possible space for such things has been closed off for good. But let's not get too nostalgic.

There is something strange about the absence of women talking from cinema. Aren't women supposed to always be talking? Of course, they're not meant to be talking about anything *important*, which is presumably why the camera only turns to them when men are mentioned. Kant in his *Anthropology* (1798) is quite bothered by women's 'loquacity', mentioning it several times, particularly when it goes 'wrong':

Amentia (*Unsinnigkeit*) is the inability to bring one's represen-tations into even the coherence necessary for the possibility of experience. In lunatic asylums it is women who, owing to their talkativeness, are most subject to this disease: that is, their lively power of imagination inserts so much into what they are relating that no one grasps what they actually wanted to say.[40]

Too much talking prevents even the possibility of experience – no space/time for you, girly, you just sit there in the corner and babble crazily to yourself! It's not that women think just about men, it's that they think about everything, madly, all the time. How could cinema possible deal with *that*?

Films that appear to be 'all about women', such as *Sex and the City* are paeans to a curious combination of ultra-mediation and a post-religious obsession with 'the one'. You go to 'the City' in search of 'labels and love'; the one mediating the other – the nicest thing your boyfriend can do for you is have a giant wardrobe installed for all your 'labels'. Drinks with 'the girls' are dominated by discussions about whether he is 'the one' or not. What does this obsession with 'the one' mean? The bourgeoisie may have drowned the most heavenly ecstasies of religious fervor, of chivalrous enthusiasm, of philistine sentimentalism, in the icy water of egotistical calculation, as Marx and Engels observed, but certain religious motifs are harder to shake than others. The 'one' as the transcendent culmination of an entire romantic destiny demonstrates a curious mélange of the senti-mental ('we were always meant to be together!') and the cynical (if there's a 'one' then the 'non-ones' don't count; the sex with them is of no importance, there is no need to behave even moder-ately pleasantly towards them). Marriage, for example, for many is still something other than a mere contract. But this strange mix of sentimentality and pragmatism – ideology, if ever there were a definition – reproduces itself seemingly spontaneously, in culture and conversation.

There is no emancipation here, if all effort is ultimately

retotalized onto the project of 'the one'; if all discussions with 'friends' are merely mediating stepping-stones in the eschatological fulfillment of romantic purpose. Contemporary cinema is profoundly conservative in this regard; and the fact that it both reflects and dictates modes of current behavior is depressingly effective, and effectively depressing.

Perhaps the only thing worse than wondering about what women are talking about is seeing them actually do it, at least as far as *Sex And The City* goes. If cinema tends to show women talking to each other only about men (or marriage, or babies) perhaps the most important aspect of this is *brevity*. An entire film given over to such things would be obscene according to the logic of mainstream cinema, which can barely tolerate a few minutes of such footage, even in its 'unambiguously flattering' mode. I think this is indicated by the common observation that men feel alienated and frustrated by an hour or so of *Sex and the City*. A winsome few moments of love-lorn anguish shared between two friends is ok, lengthy discussions of fellatio are not.

Mainstream cinema mediates the relationship between men through the odd woman, who rarely gets to mediate anything at all through anyone or anything else. But in the 'real world' do women mediate their relationships through discussion of men? One could ask a similar question about make-up and fashion. Prettifying for the boys or warning signs for the other ladies? Obviously the idea that straight women are constantly 'competing' for men is an awful one, but they are most definitely supposed to, according to the crazy logic of scarcity that consumerism depends upon. He's the one! That handbag is the one! Hands off my bag/man!

Between the world of work and the consumerism of contemporary culture, and the feminism that justifies it, lies an industry that best synthesizes the two, and it is to this that we now turn. Of all the industries most symbolic of the death of interiority and the centrality of sex, pornography is the one that stands out most, *or at least got there first.* The 'pornification' of contemporary life has often been noted, but too often the discussion takes place in moral terms. It is much more interesting and relevant to think of pornography as a particular kind of work, indeed, as a paradigmatic mode of work.

3.0 Pornography as a Privileged Mode of Work

Pornography has historically split feminism along political lines. Andrea Dworkin famously made allegiances with right-wing groups who shared her hatred of pornography, if not any of her other positions. More recent feminism has tended to regard it more benignly, particularly if it is deemed to be of an 'emancipatory' variety, if it falls on along the line that runs from vibrators to pole-dancing to 'feeling sexy'. Both positions frame the issue in moral terms – pornography is either degrading therefore bad *or* it is enjoyable and thus morally good. But pornography is, we must first of all acknowledge, a massive industry with major economic and social import. It is also an industry with its own self-perpetuating culture, one that has trouble remembering its own history, unless there is money to be made from 'retro' footage. It often seems disgusted with itself, with its own past, as the pornographic mode of production seeks to close in on itself and deny its own parentage. After all, porn-sex is barren sex. The various media of porn (literature, photographs, film) and the channels of distribution (dramatically increased with the arrival of Web 2.0) refuse to look back. The following section juxtaposes contemporary pornography with earlier cinematic examples to point out not only that pornography has changed quite radically, but further that its future need not be as grim as its present. Tracing the origins of certain contemporary forms of pornography back through a part of its early cinematic history, shows that we can analyze porn not only in terms of its immediate effects on its viewers (as if these are easily discernible anyway) but in terms of the ways it organizes the senses differently over time. By looking at the origins of cinematic pornography we can learn much about the way we understand porn tropes today, and precisely, despite all the 'choice', what we're missing.

It seems clear that there is a break in cinematic pornography that happens in the post-World War II period. One place that we see this change – in this case a direct reflection of the rapid rise in consumerism in the 1950s and 60s – is in the altered relation of sexuality to objects in porn films during the period; namely, the rise of the sex toy as prop. At the same time, as one can see in examples of the American 'stag' film of the 1950s, there is a switch from the viewer as voyeur on a private scene to the viewer as explicitly addressed by the participants in the film. It is as if John Berger's claim about painting in *The Ways of Seeing*, namely that 'almost all post-Renaissance European sexual imagery is frontal – either literally or metaphorically – because the sexual protagonist is the spectator-owner looking at it,'[41] is recapitulated in cinematic pornography – only this time at an accelerated pace such that the change occurs over the course of a few decades rather than several centuries. It is no surprise that this turn to the viewer coincides with the reduction in sexual participants on camera. In pre-1950s pornography films, there is a tendency for many characters to enter the stage, in various combinations (combinations that would be broken up these days into gay porn/straight porn/real lesbian porn/lesbian porn for men, etc, etc.).

However, one should be wary of presenting an overly cumulative story about the development (and qualitative if not quantitative decline) of pornography. It is not simply the case that we move from an open to a closed, albeit multiple, model.

Rather the history of pornography should be understood diachronically – the murals at Pompeii depicting the atomization of sex acts (one room for fellatio, one room for men together, one room for women together, one for men and women, etc.) has more in common with the current segregation of fetishes/kinks than the rather more bacchanalian free-for-all of some of the early porn films.

Porn today deploys sex as something to be treated outside of other human and social relations, even as it depicts 'office sex', 'teacher sex', 'cop sex', etc. This is very much unlike pornography at other points in history, such as during the French Revolution, where it was used as a way of attacking the monarchy and the established order. Similarly the prostitute of 18th century novels is often a sort of organic materialist philosopher as well as a debunker of the hypocrisy of conventional society – for it is she who knows the truth about how things 'really work', politically and scientifically. Both those who defend pornography on the grounds of free speech, and those, such as Dworkin and MacKinnon, who come down strongly against porn, take as their model a debased, one-sided representation of desire and thus treat porn as if it were a historical invariant, one which always has the same kind of content. The ahistoricism of the anti-pornography movement takes as its presupposition the idea that men will always nurture a violent desire towards women and that porn is merely a reflection of this. As Dworkin puts it 'The insult pornography offers, invariably, to sex is accomplished in the active subordination of women: the creation of a sexual dynamic in which the putting-down of women, and ultimately the brutalization of women, *is* what sex is taken to be.'[42] Making pornography a free speech issue similarly obscures the historical specificity of porn at any given moment. The ahistorical approach to pornography neglects to consider the social and economic conditions surrounding both the form and content of pornography as it exists at any given time.

There is no doubt that the porn uppermost in Dworkin's mind was the often extremely nasty, violent porn of the 1970s, and that the exploitation of women in a porn industry was as brutal and any other in the increasingly neo-liberal and unjust society of American capitalism. But this is precisely the point. Violence, and the violence specific to certain kinds of pornography cannot be completely removed from a complete analysis of the society that produces it. As Wendy Brown puts it with reference to MacKinnon's work:

> MacKinnon's move to read gender off of pornography, her construction of a social theory of gender that mirrors hetero-sexual male pornography, not only convenes a pervasively, totally, and singly determined gendered subject, it encodes the pornographic age as the truth rather than the hyperbole of gender production.[43]

If we take instead a historical approach, one might even say a dialectical approach, towards pornography, then we might want to look to a different kind of archive, that of vintage porn, as a way out of the 'porn good'/'porn bad' opposition. In that sense, then, the argument about pornography is ultimately a positive one, taking up Angela Carter's point that:

> Pornographers are the enemies of women only because of our contemporary ideology of pornography does not encompass the possibility of change, as if we were the slaves of history and not its makers, as if sexual relations were not necessarily an expression of social relations, as if sex itself were an external fact, one as immutable as the weather, creating human practice but never a part of it.[44]

It is useful and revealing to compare contemporary porn to older forms to see if there are any resources for Carter's suggestion that pornography could potentially participate fully in human practice.

3.1 The Money Shot: Pornography and Capitalism

The sheer *hard work* of contemporary porn informs you that, without delusion, sex is just like everything else – grinding, relentless, boring (albeit *multiply* boring). The pneumatic Calvinism of rubberized piston porn-duty, the grim orgasm of unsmiling physical moil. But sex-as-work is the lesser partner in the invention of porn-capitalism. Where does it all end up, after all but in *the money shot*. The trajectory of the money shot is the history not only of filmed pornography (a contradiction in terms given the 'graphy' of the original medium – the 'writing of/about prostitutes' in the name of a social materialism that sought to bring down the church alongside its concomitant bourgeois hypocrisy), but also the sheer explosive pointlessness of capital itself, abasing itself in a repeated act of onanism that blinds and silences the other in a gobbet of slightly disappointing sexual-Tippex.

Oppose to this the short, silent black-and-white films from around the 1910s to the 1950s. They are overwhelmingly French, because of advances in French cinematography and relatively lax censorship laws compared to Britain and Germany at the time. These films were generally screened privately or in the waiting-rooms of brothels, in order to excite the client and make the prostitute's job a little quicker. A recent collection of silent porno-graphic films, mostly made in France between 1905 and 1930 and collected by French director Michael Reilhac as 'The Good Old Naughty Days', astonishes for several reasons.

The first thing you notice in these early films is the sheer level of silliness on show: sex isn't just a succession of grim orgasms and the parading of physical prowess, but something closer to slapstick and vaudeville. Men pretend to be statues of fauns for curious women to tickle; two seamstresses fall into a fit of giggles as their over-excited boss falls off the bed; a bawdy waitress serves a series of sexually-inspired meals to a man dressed as a musketeer before joining him for 'dessert'. This kind of theatrical role-play prefigures many of the clichés of contemporary pornography, of course: nuns, school-mistresses, the 'peeping tom' motif, and so on. But the beauty of these early short films lies in the details, the laughter of its participants and the sheer variety of the bodies on parade: the unconventionally attractive mingle with the genuinely pretty; large posteriors squish overjoyed little men. The fact that the rules of pornographic film-making haven't yet been formally established, as well as the rudimentary nature of the film equipment, means that often the filming cuts off before any sort of climax, which only adds to the amateurish, unstructured, anarchic charm of it all.

The attitude towards sex in these early pornographic efforts is closer to the mordant humor of Samuel Beckett than the action-film over-kill of *Suck It Dry 3* and its ilk. As the narrator of *Malone Dies* recounts:

> And though both were completely impotent they finally succeeded, summoning to their aid all the resources of the skin, the mucus and the imagination, in striking from their dry and feeble clips a kind of somber gratification.[45]

One should not imagine, though, that all that vintage porn presents is the odd dirty kiss or flash of thigh. In fact, some of the footage in the Reilhac collection is so explicit that it received a

R18 rating (a classification for films deemed even more explicit than those that would usually fall under the 18 category).

What shocks the contemporary audience more than any of the specific acts on display, however, is the fact that the participants genuinely seem to be enjoying themselves, and that they might even be quite keen on sleeping with each other. Furthermore, for all the shouting and screaming of contemporary porn, it's rare to see a woman smile, or laugh: vintage pornography abounds in sweet expressions and moments of shared affection. The polymorphous perversity of the actors reminds us that sex can be both witty, but also that it's not a competition – many of the short films from the early twentieth century involve the inability of men to achieve erection and the increasingly comical attempts of their remarkably understanding lovers to try to amend the situation. The humanist promise of early cinema seems to have been betrayed by a combination of artificial and destructive antagonisms between men and women and unnecessary anxieties about 'performance' and desirability.

One of the most interesting things about so-called 'vintage erotica', for all its indifference to the well-timed cut, its wasteful expenditure in the pursuit of female pleasure, and so on is the presence of the 'money shot' (of course, this term too is now rather coy – we mean *cum shot* surely). It is initially surprising – the money shot seems like it should have been a recent invention, something suited to a more hyper-real, obsessively graphic age, but there it is, all over the 1920s, as if the logic of the tension between make-believe and authenticity has already been encoded for the big porn Other.

The money shot has always been about different kinds of 'money', however. It's not clear whether the mainstream meaning of 'money shot' (literally, the most expensive scene in the film) got transplanted to porn or vice versa: the money shot these days is just as likely to be the action hero's virile escape from a terrorist-induced explosion as a guy trying his best to 'put out'. But the porn meaning is complex: is it the point at which the guy completes his 'product' and thus makes the thing he gets paid for, in a base capitalist form? But where, then, is the alienation here? (And we should bear in mind that porn is one of the only industries in which men usually get paid less than women.) Or is it, instead, the point at which the audience 'get their money's worth?' in the sense that what has been delivered to them has finally, irrevocably been proved to be 'real': 'oh my God, honey, they really did it!'

This passion for authenticity, which unsurprisingly works even better as the only-ever-hinted-at 'real' sex-scene of the mainstream film, is curious: is it not enough that we see and hear 'pleasure' on the face of the participants? Of course not – just like any other woman, the porn actress could be faking it. But there is no way of measuring her pleasure, of course, even though vintage porn does its best to assure us that female jouissance has its own place. But the money shot has moved again – from mainstream cinema, to porn, to TV – in this last context it is used to describe the key scene in a reality show that provides a kind of low-level climax for the programme to hook the trailer on: a clip of a contestant breaking down and crying during his or her post-elimination, or falling, or screaming. Even money can sometimes get cheaper.

In keeping with the varieties of linguistic invention inherent to porn, indeed the very desire for the image to keep up with language, there has to be an ever-increasingly specific remit internal to porn classification itself – not just 'facials', but 'eye-shots', 'ear-shots', 'mouth-shots'. One of the things about early 20th-century erotic photography, on the other hand, is its lack of taxonomy. Contemporary pornography has more categories than there are dirty thoughts in the world, and yet it fails in one crucial respect – it can no longer surprise. You could be into women who look like cats who specialize in shaving biscuits whilst bouncing up and down on trampolines, and there'd probably be a website that could cater to your needs, but once you've seen a couple of cat-women shaving biscuits whilst bouncing on trampolines *surely you've seen them all*. The excessive taxonomical drive of contemporary pornography is merely one element of its quest to bore us all to death and remind us that everything is merely a form of work, including, or even most especially, pleasure.[46]

With the introduction of sex toys in the 1950s (the vibrator, but also the radio, the telephone, the television), porn becomes radically miserable. Women sit alone in houses filled with consumer goods, popping out only to purchase the biggest vibrator they can find. Occasionally they might flick through a book, or more likely, a magazine, but it never distracts them for long. Unlike the comedic role-play of twenties and thirties porn, or the frenetic war-apocalypse porn of the 1940s, Fifties European porn looks like a cross between a Godard film in which women hang around looking a bit bored (most of them surely are) and a rape fantasy. In a final, psychotic twist, one of the short 1950s films, 'The Demon of Boredom', involves a listless housewife inviting over the sex-shop owner who has just sold her a vibrator. Once at her place, she spikes his aperitif and orally rapes him with the same dildo while he sits unconscious in her chair. The toy is both bizarrely emancipatory and shockingly alienating.

Flash forward fifty years and we can ask what would a non-alienated contemporary pornography look like? Chances are that even the most adamant defender of the charms of adult material would struggle to find much evidence of compassion or affection in today's relentlessly lurid output. Contemporary pornography informs us of one thing above all else: sex is a type of work, just like any other. What matters most is quantity – the bigger the better. It is not for nothing that one of the most successful sex videos of all time, starring Annabel Chong, features 251 sex acts performed with approximately 70 men during a ten hour period. Contemporary pornography is realistic only in the sense that it sells back to us the very worst of our aspirations: domination, competition, greed and brutality.

The pornography industry itself is a veritable juggernaut, generating an estimated $57 billion in annual revenue worldwide. It makes more money than Hollywood and all major league sports put together. 300,000 internet sites are currently devoted to its propagation, and 200 new films are estimated to be made every week. Almost any genre and type of sexual taste is catered for, just so long as you aren't looking for anything as recherché as sweetness or wit.

On one level, we might say, so what? Pornography serves a certain practical purpose, why expect anything more from it? If you want romance, go and read Mills and Boon! Alternatively, we might side with anti-pornography feminists and argue that the genre is so irredeemably associated with violence and misogyny that we should steer well clear of it, and perhaps even campaign for its abolition. But what if there was another history of porn, one that was filled less with pneumatic shaven bodies pummeling each other into submission than with sweetness, silliness and bodies that didn't always function and purr like a well-oiled machine? The early origins of cinematic pornography tell a very different story about the representation of sex, one that suggests a way both out of the rubberized inhumanity of today's hardcore obsession, but also out of the claim that pornography is inherently exploitative. But pornography alone tells us nothing unless we accept Angela Carter's argument that there is an intimate link between sexual relations and social relations.

3.2 Socialism Must Not Exclude Human Sensual Pleasure From Its Program!

Despite the claim that 'there is no such thing as too much fun', plastered all over the dirty Teflon of the reopened Millennium Dome, we must sadly come to terms with the fact that we live in a world in which enjoyment has been profoundly circumscribed. Don't be misled: The imperative to 'Enjoy!' is omnipresent, but pleasure and happiness are almost entirely absent. We can have as many vibrators as we like, and drink as much booze as we can physically tolerate, but anything else outside the echo chamber of money-possessions-pleasure is strictly verboten. Communes, you say! Collectives! Alternative models of the family! What are you, *mad*?! It's a weary indictment of the state of things when virtually every book on these topics has been removed from your university library. People can't possibly have once thought that there might be more to life than Daddy-Mummy-Me...*could they*?

Whatever *did* happen to those dreams of living differently? To the radical Kibbutzim, co-housing groups, revolutionary cells? When the 'queer' comes to stand in for the right for everyone to own their own fuck-pad, and the family turns ever inward upon itself ('now we've finally managed to save up for a mortgage, how about we schedule in a child around 2010?'), when gay lifestyle magazines fill their pages with advice on how best to marry and adopt you know the restoration is truly upon us. Alternative living these days is more likely to refer to the fact that you've bolted a solar panel to your roof rather than undertaken any practical critique of the nuclear family.

Thus we move, just like theories of Being in Medieval theology, from the many (a generalized sexual hedonia) to the one (the 'life partner' who agrees to share the mortgage) but with nothing in between, apart, perhaps, for some, a fleeting glimpse of possible alternatives. But the shared student house, or squatting with an anarchist group or pottering off for a few years to an ashram in one's early twenties are scarcely more than temporary diversions, slotted in to an already pre-ordained telos of domestic and economic stability. They lack structure – and *deliberately* so.

Dušan Makavejev's *WR: Mysteries of the Organism* and *The Switchboard Operator*, whilst in strong part a metaphorical portrayal of the abusive relationship between the Soviet Union and Yugoslavia, simultaneously poses the question of what it might be to have a different attitude towards sex, and as a corollary to this, what it would be to live differently, to think beyond the apparently all-pervasive political separation of family and the world. What if every fuck was a kind of communism, egalitarian, joyful and for the good of all? This would precisely not be communalism, a kind of withdrawn fellowship, but a re-establishment of the link between sex and politics. This is the link that capitalism needs to obfuscate in order to hide its true dependency on the ordering and regulation of reproduction. The family in this sense is always precisely a question of the relationship between sex and politics, how it is that someone first arrives at the gates of the labor market in the first place and subsequently remains fit and functioning enough to sell eight hours of their labor power a day. But the increasing dominance of the ideology of domesticity, shored up by endless televisual imperatives to clean, decorate or sell your home, increasingly strips all living arrangements, whether they be the single flat set up for a series of one-night stands or the nuclear household with kids and a puppy in the garden, of their real political status. While one of the lasting achievements of feminism is to re-establish the link between household labor, reproductive labor and paid labor, capitalism has to perpetually pretend that the world of politics has nothing to do with the home.

3.3 From Sexoleftism to Deflationary Acceptance

There are perhaps two alternative ways of politicizing sex, neither of which is particularly satisfactory. The first takes sex as being itself inherently liberatory. Makavejev's films flirt with the powerful energies of a liberated sexuality, with particular reference to Reich, but tend to turn nasty when the question of what it would be to prolong such a project arises. When we look to actual attempts to put Reich's ideas into practice, in projects such as Otto Mühl's 1970s Viennese commune, we see one of the problems of something like an overpoliticization of sex, an overcentralization of its importance that eventually (inevitably?) leads to new forms of domination. Mühl's ambitions for eventually realizing a free society began with the declaration of war on one enemy in particular: monogamy. It was rather a popular choice, as by 1972 hundreds had joined his commune and other sections were set up all over Germany.

Rather than our current many-then-one model, Mühl attempted something like a simple substitution – life-long fidelity was to be replaced by absolute promiscuity. Members were forbidden to have sex with the same partner more than once a week, yet all must have sex five times a day – romantic love was deemed bourgeois, foreplay old-fashioned. Sex was to be performed as quickly and mechanically as possible. The Weather Underground had their own militant version of this sexual critique of bourgeois morality: marathon criticism sessions, fuelled by LSD, which included forcing members of the group with no sexual attraction to each other to have sex, or making the boyfriend of one member watch his girlfriend have sex with another man. What is being invoked here is kind of sexual cognitive dissonance designed to shore up commitment to the group and ensure total subjective (and sexual) destitution. No more romantic dreams.

The anxieties and inequalities of desire seem to always rear their ugly head, however: not all members of the commune are equally desirable, some are in fact very undesirable, and one person in particular is incredibly desirable, Mühl himself, who takes on an increasingly phallic status. Hierarchy returns as the select few super-attractive people extricate themselves from the desires of the rabble. Predictably, sexoleftism rapidly turned into a tyranny of copulation as Mühl is later accorded *droit de seigneur* over every young girl who 'comes of age'. Mühl was eventually sentenced in the 1980s to seven years in jail for child sex offences.

The central problem of the notion of sex as inherently egalitarian emerges when it turns out that desire isn't fair at all. Accepting the notion that desire is a tyrant forms the second attempt to link sex and politics: we could call this the tragic-psychoanalytic model, which at least has the virtue of speaking intelligently about itself. If there is no sexual relation, there is certainly no possibility of founding a community upon it, unless, precisely, it is a *collective which is not one.*

The problem here is twofold: first, the relative ahistoricality of this model of sex, as if all maladapted animals with this peculiar relation to language will always wear their desire like a damaged mark of shame. The second problem involves the proximity of the tragic-psychoanalytic model's conception of sex to the practical bourgeois performance of sex: here there really is no sexual relation! Only an economic, ossified and status-based one. Between isolationist sexual utopianism and a wry displacement of the importance of sex lies a poorly served desire for a collective sexuality that neither makes sex the be-all-and-end-all (as it were) nor a dirty little secret to be drowned in proprietary and hypocritical moralizing.

The family too invariably compromises communalistic aspirations. Some early radical kibbutzim were self-enclosed, i.e. they hadn't factored in reproduction at all. When babies started arriving they had to quickly adapt. On one level, this seems laughable – what were they thinking? But on another, it makes perfect sense. A commune could easily sustain itself with a steady flow of members from the outside – although this would depend upon a certain parasitism. Still, the question of families has not yet been adequately resolved. Their dark heart bubbles to the surface all too often:

> Murderous mothers and incestuous fathers, who are infinitely more widespread than pedophile killers, are an unsettling intrusion into the idyllic portrait of the family, which depicts the delightful relationship between our citizen parents and their angelic offspring.[47]

Revelations with regards to the way in which 'citizen parents' can sometimes treat their children remind us, as if we needed reminding, that families, when they go wrong, go really *really* wrong.

Badiou in *The Century* attempts to reawaken the original impulse of Freud's thought by reminding us that 'he explained human thought on the basis of child sexuality' and that 'there is nothing either natural or obvious about the fact that the object of desire for a subject is borne by the opposite sex'. Both the 'naturalness' of heterosexuality and the sexual innocence of the child are simultaneously put into question by psychoanalysis, and it is Badiou's conviction that Freud's attempt to address the 'real of sex, rather than its meaning' has sadly become lost in the ubiquitous call for mandatory, yet hyper-moralized, enjoyment.

Badiou seems somewhat depressed about sex, in fact, and certainly not pleased with pornography ('Bénazéraf has not kept any of his promises'), despite the fact that it supposedly touches on the 'very essence of cinema insofar as it is confronted with the full visibility of the sexual'.[48] Nowhere do we find a communist hypothesis with regard to the future uses of a sexuality that responds to the insights of psychoanalysis in a non-hysterical manner.

For that we must turn to the deplorably overlooked Shulamith Firestone and her 1970 tract, *The Dialectic of Sex*. In the final chapter, 'The Ultimate Revolution', Firestone takes seriously the implications of what she calls 'cybernetic communism', the total emancipation of women (and men) from the shackles of biology via advances in contraceptive, reproductive technology and alternative models of work and social organization ('Natural childbirth is only one more part of the reactionary hippie-Rousseauean Return-to-Nature'). Not surprisingly, she ends up touching on the same 'real' of sex as Freud, that of child sexuality, only instead of merely noting it (shocking enough in the first place, admittedly), she attempts to incorporate it into her plans for a future utopia of collectives, work-replacing machines and no more 'natural' pregnancy.

Following the 'complete integration' of 'sexegrated' women and children into society, Firestone argues that we will uncover 'for the first time', *natural* sexual freedom (intriguingly technologism is the precondition for humanist practice). The sexual freedom of all women and children is summarized baldly in the following way: 'now they can do whatever they wish to do sexually': Cybernetics simply destroys the incest taboo. Relations with children would include, apparently, 'as much genital sex as the child was capable of ... but because genital sex would no longer be the central focus of the relationship, lack of orgasm would not present a serious problem.'[49] This idea of the *literal* limits of child sexuality is extreme, though not without its historical echoes in the intellectual climate of the time ('Certain children opened the flies of my trousers and started to tickle me,' said Daniel Cohn-Bendit. 'I reacted differently each time, according to the circumstances ... But when they insisted on it, I then caressed them.'[50]) The immediate cry of 'pedophile!' is enough to put a very rapid end to this kind of sexual utopianizing both in theory and in practice, but 'the problem of children', as Foucault puts it, remains very much with us, a creepy secret in the basement of an otherwise perfectly normal-looking family house.

A recent news story, concerning a supposed 'pregnancy pact' between a group of Massachusetts teenage girls, is interesting, far less for the scurrilous details (they slept with the same 24-year-old homeless guy! We blame *Juno*!), than for the conditions of the pact.[51] This was not merely a bid to individually break the boredom of adolescence, but a desire to raise the babies 'collectively'. Aside from any supposed moral repugnance at such a project, this isn't actually such a stupid idea. If you're going to have kids, you might as well have them young, and divide up the labor. What's the point of individually washing one sick-covered baby outfit when you could wash twenty at once?

There is a moral/biological paradox here: physically it makes much more sense to have a kid when you are still relatively fit. 30/40-something mothers with decades of boozing, dieting and stress may be better placed financially, but they certainly aren't as able to bounce back from weeks of sleeplessness like a 15-year-old netball playing girl would be. But no nice middle class parent is going to put university on hold for the child of their child. Just as the school superintendent said of the girls in the pact: 'They are young white women. We understand that some of them were together talking about being pregnant and that being a positive thing for them.' The horror! But, but...they're white! And they want to do it! It's easier to imagine the end of the world than it is to imagine the death of the nuclear family.

But sometimes the things that look the hardest have the simplest answers. When Toni Morrison was asked in an interview in *Time* about pregnancy twenty years ago, she gave the following responses. They deserve reprinting at length:

Q. This leads to the problem of the depressingly large number of single-parent households and the crisis in unwed teenage pregnancies. Do you see a way out of that set of worsening circumstances and statistics?

A. Well, neither of those things seems to me a debility. I don't think a female running a house is a problem, a broken family. It's perceived as one because of the notion that a head is a man.

Two parents can't raise a child any more than one. You need a whole community — everybody — to raise a child. The notion that the head is the one who brings in the most money is a patriarchal notion, that a woman — and I have raised two children, alone — is somehow lesser than a male head. Or that I am incomplete without the male. This is not true. And the little nuclear family is a paradigm that just doesn't work. It doesn't work for white people or for black people. Why we are hanging onto it, I don't know. It isolates people into little units — people need a larger unit.

Q. And teenage pregnancies?

A. Everybody's grandmother was a teenager when they got pregnant. Whether they were 15 or 16, they ran a house, a farm, they went to work, they raised their children.

Q. But everybody's grandmother didn't have the potential for living a different kind of life. These teenagers — 16, 15 — haven't had time to find out if they have special abilities, talents. They're babies having babies.

A. The child's not going to hurt them. Of course, it is absolutely time consuming. But who cares about the schedule? What is this business that you have to finish school at 18? They're not babies. We have decided that puberty extends to what — 30? When do people stop being kids? The body is ready to have babies, that's why they are in a passion to do it. Nature wants it done then, when the body can handle it, not after 40, when the income can handle it.

Q. You don't feel that these girls will never know whether they could have been teachers, or whatever?

A. They can be teachers. They can be brain surgeons. We have to help them become brain surgeons. That's my job. I want to take them all in my arms and say, 'Your baby is beautiful and so are you and, honey, you can do it. And when you want to be a brain surgeon, call me — I will take care of your baby.' That's the attitude you have to have about human life. But we don't want to pay for it.

I don't think anybody cares about unwed mothers unless they're black — or poor. The question is not morality, the question is money. That's what we're upset about. We don't care whether they have babies or not.

Q. How do you break the cycle of poverty? You can't just hand out money.

A. Why not? Everybody gets everything handed to them. The rich get it handed — they inherit it. I don't mean just inheritance of money. I mean what people take for granted among the middle and upper classes, which is nepotism, the old-boy network. That's shared bounty of class.[52]

4.0 Conclusion

The political imagination of contemporary feminism is at a standstill. The perky, upbeat message of self-fulfillment and consumer emancipation masks a deep inability to come to terms with serious transformations in the nature of work and culture. For all its glee and excitement, the self-congratulatory feminism that celebrates individual identity above all else is a one-dimensional feminism. It is the flip-side of the image of the one-dimensional worker who is expected never to let herself or her company down by dressing badly, not being enthusiastic or, worst of all, getting pregnant. The feminization of labor and the laborization of women will continue to run adrift on the major contradictions of capitalism and the opportunistic sexism that accompanies it, and no amount of sticking-plaster pleasures will compensate.

The sheer crystalline simplicity of Morrison's insights into the relationship between class, race and gender, and the memory that sex, cinema and alternative modes of living once held great promise, should remind us that feminism was at one time a great generator of new thoughts and new modes of existence. With the shattering of certain economic 'certainties' comes the questioning of other supposedly 'natural' modes of behavior. If feminism takes this opportunity to shake off its current imperialist and consumerist sheen it could once again place its vital transformative political demands centre-stage, and shuffle off its current one-dimensionality for good.

Endnotes

1. Herbert Marcuse, One-Dimensional Man, (Boston: Beacon Press, 1964), p. 25.
2. Paolo Virno, 'Post-Fordist Semblance', SubStance, Issue 112 (Vol. 36, no. 1), 2007, p. 42.
3. Lindsey German, Material Girls: Women, Men and Work (London: Bookmarks, 2007), p. 148.
4. Zillah Eistenstein, Sexual Decoys: Gender, Race and War In Imperial Democracy (London: Zed Books, 2007), p. xviii.
5. See Eisenstein's argument that 'poor black women make up the greatest numbers of people living below sea level without cars' in the affected region. Sexual Decoys, p. 80.
6. http://www.lacan.com/jampalin.html
7. http://www.guardian.co.uk/commentisfree/2008/sep/12/sarahpalin.feminism
8. See Katharine Viner's 'Feminism as Imperialism': http://www.guardian.co.uk/world/2002/sep/21/gender.usa
9. Sarah Palin fever has prompted a surge in sales of the shoes, spectacles and even wigs needed for her 'look". See: http://www.telegraph.co.uk/news/newstopics/uselection2008/sarahpalin/2826084/Sarah-Palin-fever-boosts-wig-sales-as-women-go-for-her-look.html
10. Laura Bush decries Taliban 'brutality', BBC, 17/11/01.
11. Katha Pollitt, 'After Iraq and Afghanistan, Muslim Feminists Are Leery of Seeming Close to the West', The Nation, 23/06/07.

12. Katherine Viner, 'Feminism as Imperialism', The Guardian, 12/09/02.
13. Ibid.
14. Alain Badiou, 'Behind the Scarfed Law, There is Fear', http://www.lacan.com/islbad.htm.
15. David Aaronovitch, 'Please Don't Rub My Face in Your Faith', The Guardian, 17/06/03.
16. 'Behind the Scarfed Law, There is Fear', op. cit.
17. Karl Marx, Capital, vol. 1 (London: Penguin, 1976), section 9.
18. Charlie Ball, Hecsu labour market analyst, quoted in http://news.bbc.co.uk/1/hi/education/4929958.stm
19. hhttp://www.statistics.gov.uk/pdfdir/lmsuk0808.pdf
20. http://news.bbc.co.uk/1/hi/business/7357509.stm
21. '100% of the ability, 60% of the pay: agency targets top women looking for flexibility', The Guardian, April 23 2007.
22. Cristina Morini, 'The Feminization of Labour in Cognitive Capitalism', Feminist Review, 87, 2007.
23. David Harvey, Spaces of Hope (Edinburgh: Edinburgh University Press, 2000), p. 103.
24. Ibid.
25. Virno, 'Post-Fordist Semblance', p. 44.
26. 'I'm a celebrity, get off with me' http://entertainment.timesonline.co.uk/tol/arts_and_enter-tainment/tv_and_radio/article524635.ece
27. From 'Up The Revolution!', Jessica Valenti, The Guardian, 18/04/07.
28. Ariel Levy, Female Chauvinist Pigs: Women and the Rise of Raunch Culture (Free Press, 2005), p. 5.
29. FCP, p. 200.
30. Jessica Valenti, Full Frontal Feminism: A Young Women's Guide to Why Feminism Matters (Seal Press, 2007), p. 1.
31. Ibid., p. 8.
32. Ibid., p. 14.
33. Ibid., p. 34.

34. Ibid., p. 39.
35. Ibid., p. 43.
36. Quoted in Female Chauvinist Pigs, p. 58.
37. http://abcnews.go.com/Technology/Story?id=2467150& page=2
38. 'Why Women Should Fake Orgasms', Fay Weldon, Daily Mail, 07/09/06.
39. http://www.antipope.org/charlie/blog-static/2008/ 07/bechdels_law.html
40. Immanuel Kant, Anthropology from a Pragmatic Point of View, Cambridge University Press (Cambridge: 2006), p. 109.
41. John Berger, Ways of Seeing, (London: Penguin, 1990), p. 56.
42. Andrea Dworkin, 'Against the Male Flood: Censorship, Pornography and Equality', Feminism and Pornography, ed. Drucilla Cornell (Oxford: Oxford University Press, 2000), p. 25.
43. Wendy Brown, 'The Mirror of Pornography', Feminism and Pornography, p. 208
44. Angela Carter, 'Pornography in the Service of Women', Feminism and Pornography, p. 342.
45. Samuel Beckett, Malone Dies (Grove Press, 1991), p. 261.
46. There's something both curious and creepy about the way in which porn exercises the taxonomical drive. As a student I lived with a guy who let me use his computer. What amazed me about his extensive collection of pornographic pictures culled from the net (mostly fluffy stuff like girls in velvet cuffs dressed in Santa Claus outfits) was the amount and time and effort he'd put into cataloguing his pictures (e.g. single woman: blonde: bra: heels or two women: brunette: blonde: whip, etc. etc.). Obviously, the enjoyment he derived from porn was intimately connected to the collecting itself: had the hours he put into such an enterprise been spent on his course he would have done very well, instead of dropping out. He later joined the police force.

47. Alain Badiou, 'Sex in Crisis', The Century, trans. Alberto Toscano (London: Polity, 2007), p. 75.

48. Alain Badiou, 'Philosophy and Cinema', Infinite Thought, trans. Oliver Feltham and Justin Clemens (London: Continuum, 2003), p. 116.

49. Shulamith Firestone, The Dialectic of Sex: The Case for Feminist Revolution (London: Paladin, 1970), p. 223.

50. 'Red Face for Fischer's Friend', http://www.guardian.co.uk/world/2001/feb/23/worlddispatch. jonhenley

51. 'US fears of teen "pregnancy pact"', http://news.bbc.co.uk/1/hi/world/americas/7464925.stm

52. 'The Pain of Being Black': Bonnie Angelo interviews Toni Morrison, Time, 22/05/89.

Contemporary culture has eliminated both the concept of the public and the figure of the intellectual. Former public spaces – both physical and cultural – are now either derelict or colonized by advertising. A cretinous anti-intellectualism presides, cheerled by expensively educated hacks in the pay of multinational corporations who reassure their bored readers that there is no need to rouse themselves from their interpassive stupor. The informal censorship internalized and propagated by the cultural workers of late capitalism generates a banal conformity that the propaganda chiefs of Stalinism could only ever have dreamt of imposing. Zero Books knows that another kind of discourse – intellectual without being academic, popular without being populist – is not only possible: it is already flourishing, in the regions beyond the striplit malls of so-called mass media and the neurotically bureaucratic halls of the academy. Zero is committed to the idea of publishing as a making public of the intellectual. It is convinced that in the unthinking, blandly consensual culture in which we live, critical and engaged theoretical reflection is more important than ever before.